Fruitful Mom Journal

Filled with the Spirit

Brenda Lee Gines

Dedicated to every mom.

Table of Contents

How to Use This Journal

This journal was created to help you not only read about the Fruit of the Spirit, but to live it, practice it, and grow in it daily.

Understanding the Fruit

The Fruit of the Spirit (Galatians 5:22–23) is not something you force. It is something that is formed within you as you walk with God. Each fruit reflects His character, and as you grow in Him, that fruit begins to grow in you.

This journal is designed to help you slow down, reflect deeply, and intentionally cultivate each fruit in your everyday life as a mother.

Your Weekly Flow

Each section is thoughtfully designed to guide you from reflection → awareness → action → transformation.

Weekly Challenge

Each fruit begins with a Weekly Challenge; a simple, intentional way to practice that fruit in your daily life.

These challenges are not meant to overwhelm you, but to help you:

- Be mindful in your responses
- Grow through real-life moments
- Apply truth in practical ways

Growth happens when what you learn becomes what you live. Walk along side God through this daily journey.

From the Book: Reflection Questions

These questions are pulled directly from the corresponding chapter in Fruitful Mom: Fruit of the Spirit. Reading the chapters prior to answering would help better serve you and your understanding of each question.

They are designed to help you:

- Revisit what you've learned
- Reflect on how it applies to your life
- Recognize areas of growth and stretching

Take your time here. Let your answers be honest and unfiltered.

Heart Check

This section goes deeper. The **Heart Check** is a space for personal reflection. It's where you examine what's happening beneath the surface of your inner most parts.

Here, you'll explore:

- Your thoughts
- Your reactions
- Your triggers
- Your beliefs

This is where real transformation begins. Be open and honest with yourself.

Life Application

This is where growth becomes intentional. The **Life Application** section helps you take what you've reflected on and turn it into daily action. You'll be guided to:

- Set personal intentions
- Identify practical steps
- Apply the fruit in real-life situations

Because truth practiced daily leads to lasting change.

Fruitful Notes:
Thoughts • Ideas • Doodles • Wisdom

This is your free space. A place to:

- Write freely
- Capture thoughts
- Reflect deeper
- Doodle, dream, and process

There is no structure here; just room for you to grow, release, and create.

Scriptures to Stand On

This section includes:

- Key verses from Fruitful Mom
- Additional scriptures to strengthen and encourage you

These are your anchors. Return to them when:

- You feel overwhelmed
- You need clarity
- You need strength

Let God's Word guide your thoughts and steady your heart.

A Final Encouragement

There is no right way to complete this journal. Every woman is unique and molded through different experiences.

Remember, this journal is about your walk with God and your progress in bettering yourself. Some days will feel easy. Others not-so-much. But, both are part of the process. As you continue, remember you are not striving to become something; you are allowing God to form something within you. Stay consistent. Stay open. Stay rooted. And watch the fruit grow. You got this!

Part One
LOVE is the Foundation of It All

Love: A Moment to Reflect

Love is where it all begins. Before it is seen, before it is spoken, and even before it is fully understood, love is already at work... quietly transforming the heart. As you've just read, a mother's love reflects something far deeper: the very nature of God Himself. This kind of love is not only felt, it is chosen. It grows in the unseen places, is refined through every season, and is strengthened each time you surrender your heart to Him.

It shows up in the small, everyday moments; the patience you didn't think you had, the grace you extend when you're weary, and the quiet sacrifices no one else sees. This is the evidence of God's love working through you, gently transforming both you and the hearts entrusted to your care.

Choose love intentionally every day this week—even when it's not easy. Love is not proven in perfect moments, but in difficult ones. Make it a point to let your love be intentional, not accidental.

Below are your challenges for this week. You have seven days to complete them in any order. Place a check when you have completed the following tasks:

☐ Show your child(ren) that you love them by using words of affirmation. Focus on the little things they do right this week.

☐ Take time out of your day to play a board game with your child(ren). You'd be surprised how enjoyable it can be.

☐ Make it a point to do something with your child(ren) they have wanted to do with you, but could not.

Remember to be intentional and **Focus Daily**.

Day 1 – Speak Life
Choose your words carefully.
Replace frustration with encouragement.

Day 2 – Pause Before Reacting
When irritation rises… pause.
Respond with patience instead of impulse.

Day 3 – Serve Intentionally
Do something loving for your child that they didn't ask for.
Let love be proactive.

Day 4 – Show Affection
Hug longer. Sit closer. Be present.
Let your love be felt, not just said.

Day 5 – Forgive Quickly
Release offense immediately.
Don't let small moments grow into distance.

Day 6 – Choose Compassion
Ask: "How does God see my child right now?"
Choose compassion over correction.

Day 7 – Reflect + Reset
Look back over your week.
Where did love flow? Where did it struggle?

From the Book — Reflection Questions

1. How have you experienced God's love in motherhood: both in the beauty and in the struggle?

____

____

____

____

2. What would it look like to "put on love" more intentionally this week?

____

____

____

____

3. How can you remind yourself that love isn't lost when life feels heavy, it's simply waiting to be remembered?

____

____

____

____

4. In what areas of your daily life do you feel God inviting you to love more deeply, whether through patience, forgiveness, or compassion?

____

____

____

____

5. What truth about God's love do you need to hold onto in this season, and how can you remind yourself of it when motherhood feels heavy?

____

____

____

____

____

____

____

____

____

Heart Check

Now that you've taken a moment to reflect, allow yourself to go a little deeper.

Love is not only something we feel—it reveals the true condition of our hearts. In this space, be honest with yourself. There is no pressure here, only grace.

1. Where in your life has love been easy for you lately? Where has it been difficult?

____

____

____

2. What situations tend to test your love the most?

____

____

____

3. Have there been moments where you responded out of frustration instead of love?

____

____

____

4. Are there recurring triggers that make it harder for you to walk in love?

____

____

____

5. What thoughts or beliefs might be affecting how you give or receive love?

____

____

____

6. Have you believed any lies about yourself that impact your ability to love fully?

____

____

____

7. What area of your heart do you need to surrender to God today that is preventing you from loving freely?

____

____

____

8. Where do you need His help to love more like Him?

____

____

____

Life Application

Take what you've learned today and begin to live it out intentionally. Growth happens when truth is practiced daily.

1. Today I will...

____

____

____

2. One small way I can show this fruit...

____

____

____

3. Who needs this from me?

____

____

____

4. How can I grow in love with intention?

____

____

____

Fruitful Notes
Thoughts ♥ Ideas ♥ Doodles ♥ Wisdom

These are the truths rooted in this chapter. Return to them, speak them, and stand on them throughout your week.

Love is patient, love is kind. It does not envy, it does not boast, it is not proud. It does not dishonor others, it is not self-seeking, it is not easily angered, it keeps no record of wrongs. Love does not delight in evil but rejoices with the truth. It always protects, always trusts, always hopes, always perseveres.
(1 Corinthians 13:4–7)

For You created my inmost being; You knit me together in my mother's womb.

(Psalm 139:13)

And over all these virtues put on love, which binds them all together in perfect unity.

(Colossians 3:14)

But the fruit of the Spirit is love, joy, peace, forbearance, kindness, goodness, faithfulness, gentleness and self-control. Against such things there is no law.

(Galatians 5:22)

Do everything in love.

(1 Corinthians 16:14)

Add Any Other Bible Verse that the Lord has Impressed upon your Heart

Part Two
JOY is Finding Light in the Chaos

Joy: A Moment to Reflect

Joy is deeper than a feeling. It is not dependent on perfect moments or peaceful days, but is found in the steady presence of God within you, even in the chaos, the noise, and the unexpected turns of motherhood. Joy fills your heart.

As you've just read, a mother's joy is not rooted in circumstances, but in connection... connection to God, to purpose, and to the beauty woven into everyday moments. It is a strength that carries you and a reminder that God is near. This kind of joy is not something you chase, it is something you receive. It grows when you shift your focus, choose gratitude, and invite God into both the ordinary and the overwhelming.

Choose joy intentionally every day this week—even when it feels out of reach. Joy is not found in perfect circumstances, but in God's presence within them. This week, let your joy be rooted, not reactive.

Below are your challenges for this week. You have seven days to complete them in any order. Place a check when you have completed the following tasks:

☐ Write down one thing everyday this week that brought you and your children joy. *(What made you laugh or smile?)*

☐ Take time to rejoice in song, dance, and/or prayer 3 times this week with your children; just to celebrate God.

☐ Practice putting on joy, at least one time, by smiling and/or laughing when you find yourself in a situation where your emotions just want to scream or bottle up.

Remember to be intentional and **Focus Daily**.

Day 1 – Speak Gratitude
Start your day by thanking God first.
Let gratitude shift your perspective.

Day 2 – Shift your Focus to Blessings
When frustration rises... pause.
Refuse to let temporary moments steal your joy.

Day 3 – Smile On Purpose
Even when it's hard—choose to smile.
Joy is sometimes a decision before it becomes a feeling.

Day 4 – Celebrate Small Wins
Find joy in the little things—laughter, quiet, connection.
Let your heart notice what matters.

Day 5 – Choose Praise Over Complaining
Catch yourself before complaining.
Replace it with praise, even in imperfect moments.

Day 6 – Spread Joy to Others
Encourage someone. Lift someone up.
Joy multiplies when it's given away.

Day 7 – Reflect + Rejoice
Look back over your week.
Where did you experience joy? When did you fight for it?

From the Book — Reflection Questions

1. When was the last time you felt pure joy, and what happened at that moment?

____

____

____

____

2. How do you usually respond when joy feels far away? How might God be inviting you to find it differently?

____

____

____

____

3. Have you mistaken busyness for fruitfulness? How could slowing down make more room for joy?

____

____

____

____

4. In what ways has gratitude helped you uncover joy in your daily life?

____

____

____

____

____

____

5. How might your children experience joy through you, even on days when you don't feel it yourself?

____

____

____

____

____

____

____

____

____

Heart Check

Now that you've taken a moment to reflect, allow yourself to go a little deeper.

Joy is not just a feeling—it reveals what we are rooted in. In this space, be honest with yourself. There is no pressure here, only grace.

1. Have there been moments where you allowed circumstances to steal your joy?

____
____
____

2. What situations tend to challenge your ability to remain joyful?

____
____
____

3. Have you found yourself focusing more on what's wrong than what's good?

____
____
____

4. Are there recurring thoughts or patterns that drain your joy?

____

____

____

5. What thoughts or beliefs might be affecting your ability to walk in joy?

____

____

____

6. Have you believed any lies that make you feel undeserving of joy or peace?

____

____

____

7. What area of your heart do you need to surrender to God in order to experience His joy more fully?

____

____

____

8. Where do you need His help to restore your joy today?

____

____

____

Life Application

Take what you've learned today and begin to live it out intentionally. Growth happens when truth is practiced daily.

1. Today I Will...

____

____

____

2. One Small Way I Can Show This Fruit...

____

____

____

3. Who Needs This From Me?

____

____

____

4. How Can I Grow In joy With Intention?

____

____

____

Fruitful
Notes
Thoughts ♥ Ideas ♥ Doodles ♥ Wisdom

These are the truths rooted in this chapter. Return to them, speak them, and stand on them throughout your week.

Nehemiah said, 'Go and enjoy choice food and sweet drinks, and send some to those who have nothing prepared. This day is holy to our Lord. Do not grieve, for the joy of the Lord is your strength.'

(Nehemiah 8:10)

May the God of hope fill you with all joy and peace as you trust in him, so that you may overflow with hope by the power of the Holy Spirit.

(Romans 15:13)

You make known to me the path of life; you will fill me with joy in your presence, with eternal pleasures at your right hand.

(Psalm 16:11)

Consider it pure joy, my brothers and sisters, whenever you face trials of many kinds, because you know that the testing of your faith produces perseverance.

(James 1:2-3)

Rejoice always, pray continually, give thanks in all circumstances; for this is God's will for you in Christ Jesus.

(1 Thessalonians 5:16-18)

Add Any Other Bible Verse that the Lord has Impressed upon your Heart

Part Three
PEACE is Guarding Your Mind and Heart

Peace: A Moment to Reflect

Peace is where the heart finds rest. Before circumstances settle, before answers come, and even before everything makes sense, peace is already present; quietly anchoring the soul. As you've just read, a mother's peace reflects something far deeper: the calming presence of God Himself. This kind of peace is not only felt, it is chosen. It grows in the hidden places, is strengthened through every challenge, and deepens each time you surrender your worries to Him.

It shows up in the stillness within the chaos. It is the steady breath in overwhelming moments, the calm that guards your heart when emotions rise, and the quiet trust that God is in control.

Choose peace intentionally every day this week—even when it's not easy. Peace is not found in perfect circumstances, but in the presence of God within you. This week, let your peace be intentional, not reactive.

Below are your challenges for this week. You have seven days to complete them in any order. Place a check when you have completed the following tasks:

☐ What can you do, at least once this week, that would give your child(ren) peace of mind? Bless them with it.

☐ Separate 5 minutes of your day,everyday, to sit outside and enjoy God's creations without any digital discractions. Just be and observe.

☐ Find a quiet place and time to sit in God's presence without speaking. Let Him do the talking and recieve.

Remember to be intentional and **Focus Daily**.

Day 1 – Pause Before Reacting

When irritation rises... pause.
Take a breath and allow peace to lead your response.

Day 2 – Surrender Control

Release what you cannot control.
Trust God with what feels overwhelming.

Day 3 – Speak Peace

Choose your words carefully.
Replace tension with calm and reassurance.

Day 4 – Create Stillness

Slow down your pace. Sit, breathe, and be present.
Let peace fill the quiet moments. Be intentional.

Day 5 – Release Worry

Give your concerns to God.
Choose trust over anxious thoughts.

Day 6 – Choose Trust Over Anxiety

Let go and let God take control.
Let peace guide how you speak and act.

Day 7 – Reflect + Reset

Look back over your week.
Where did peace remain? Where did it feel challenged?

1. What would change in your home if peace became your first response instead of your last resort?

____

____

____

____

2. How do your children see and learn peace through your reactions, tone, and routines?

____

____

____

____

3. What worries are you still trying to carry on your own that God has asked you to cast onto Him?

____

____

____

____

4. What does "putting on the Shoes of Peace" look like in your everyday life?

____

____

____

____

____

5. How might surrender, not control, bring more calm to your heart and your household?

____

____

____

____

____

____

____

____

____

Heart Check

Now that you've taken a moment to reflect, allow yourself to go a little deeper.

Peace is not only something we feel—it reflects the posture of our hearts. In this space, be still and honest with yourself. There is no pressure here, only grace.

1. Where in your life have you been experiencing peace lately? Where has it felt absent?

____

____

____

2. What situations tend to disturb your peace the most?

____

____

____

3. Have there been moments where you reacted out of stress or anxiety instead of peace?

____

____

____

4. Are there recurring triggers that make it difficult for you to remain calm and steady?

____

____

____

5. What thoughts or worries have been affecting your ability to walk in peace?

____

____

____

6. Have you been holding onto anything that is preventing you from fully trusting God?

____

____

____

7. What area of your life do you need to surrender to God in order to experience His peace?

____

____

____

8. Where do you need to trust Him more and walk in peace?

____

____

____

Life Application

Take what you've learned today and begin to live it out intentionally. Growth happens when truth is practiced daily.

1. Today I Will...

____

____

____

2. One Small Way I Can Show This Fruit...

____

____

____

3. Who Needs This From Me?

____

____

____

4. How can I grow in love with intention?

____

____

____

Fruitful Notes

Thoughts ♥ Ideas ♥ Doodles ♥ Wisdom

These are the truths rooted in this chapter. Return to them, speak them, and stand on them throughout your week.

"The peace of God, which transcends all understanding, will guard your hearts and your minds in Christ Jesus.
(Philippians 4:7)

Peace I leave with you; my peace I give you. I do not give to you as the world gives. Do not let your hearts be troubled and do not be afraid.

(John 14:27)

and with your feet fitted with the readiness that comes from the gospel of peace.

(Ephesians 6:15)

You will keep in perfect peace those whose minds are steadfast, because they trust in you.

(Isaiah 26:3)

He got up, rebuked the wind and said to the waves, Quiet! Be still!' Then the wind died down and it was completely calm.
(Mark 4:39)

Cast all your anxiety on him because he cares for you.
(1 Peter 5:7)

Add Any Other Bible Verse that the Lord has Impressed upon your Heart

Part Four
PATIENCE is Trust in Slow Bloom

Patience: A Moment to Reflect

Patience is where growth is refined. Before change is visible, before progress is felt, and even before results appear, patience is already at work; quietly strengthening the heart. As you've just read, a mother's patience reflects something far deeper: the enduring nature of God Himself.

This kind of patience is not only required, it is chosen. It grows in the waiting, it's stretched through every challenge, and deepens each moment you surrender your timing to Him. It shows up in the pauses between reactions; in the gentle response when frustration rises, in the grace extended when your strength feels low, and in the steady trust that God is working even when you cannot see it.

Choose patience intentionally every day this week—even when it's not easy. Patience is not proven in calm moments, but in the ones that stretch you. This week, let your patience be intentional, not reactive.

Below are your challenges for this week. You have seven days to complete them in any order. Place a check when you have completed the following tasks:

- [ ] At least one time, let others finish speaking without interrupting them. Show them that you value their words, even if you do not agree with them.

- [ ] When someone makes a mistake, choose to respond with understanding instead of irritation.

- [ ] Remember to believe that God's timing is perfect at least 3 times this week, especially when you're patience runs thin.

Remember to be intentional and **Focus Daily**.

Day 1 – Responding Positively

Stop and step back when angry.
Give yourself a moment to think before engaging.

Day 2 – Quiet Your Frustration

Choose your tone.
Replace frustration with calm, thoughtful responses.

Day 3 – Slow Down Your Pace

Resist the urge to rush.
Move through your day with intention, not pressure.

Day 4 – Extend Grace

Allow room for mistakes—yours and theirs.
Remember, everyone has something to work on.

Day 5 – Wait Without Complaining

In moments of delay, choose a steady heart.
Understand, patience needs time to grow.

Day 6 – Respond with Understanding

Take time to consider a different perspective.
Choose empathy over quick correction.

Day 7 – Reflect + Reset

Look back over your week.
Where did patience grow? Where was it tested?

1. Where in your life is God asking you to wait in His patience instead of worry?

____

____

____

____

2. What small daily choices could help you "wait well" instead of growing weary?

____

____

____

____

3. How does patience shape the way you respond to your children, especially on hard days?

____

____

____

____

4. What would it look like to see waiting not as delay, but as divine preperation?

____

____

____

____

____

5. How might God be strengthening your patience through what feels slow, silent, or unfinished in this season?

____

____

____

____

____

____

____

____

____

____

Heart Check

Now that you've taken a moment to reflect, allow yourself to go a little deeper.

Patience is not only something we practice—it reveals the true condition of our hearts in moments of delay, pressure, and frustration.

1. Where in your life has patience come easily lately? Where has it been difficult?

____

____

____

2. What situations tend to test your patience the most?

____

____

____

3. Have there been moments where you reacted out of frustration instead of patience?

____

____

____

4. Are there recurring triggers that make it harder for you to walk in patience?

____

____

____

5. What thoughts or beliefs might be affecting your ability to respond with patience?

____

____

____

6. Have you believed any lies that cause you to feel rushed, overwhelmed, or easily frustrated?

____

____

____

7. What area of your heart do you need to surrender to God in order to grow in patience?

____

____

____

8. Where do you need His help to respond more patiently?

____

____

____

Life Application

Take what you've learned today and begin to live it out intentionally. Growth happens when truth is practiced daily.

1. Today I will...

____

____

____

2. One small way I can show this fruit...

____

____

____

3. Who needs this from me?

____

____

____

4. How can I grow in love with intention?

____

____

____

Fruitful
Notes
Thoughts ♥ Ideas ♥ Doodles ♥ Wisdom

These are the truths rooted in this chapter. Return to them, speak them, and stand on them throughout your week.

Be patient, then, brothers and sisters, until the Lord's coming. See how the farmer waits for the land to yield its valuable crop, patiently waiting for the autumn and spring rains.
(James 5:7)

Let us not become weary in doing good, for at the proper time you will reap a harvest if you do not give up.
(Galatians 6:9)

Wait for the Lord; be strong and take heart and wait for the Lord.
(Psalm 27:14)

There is a time for everything, and a season for every activity under the heavens:

(Ecclesiastes 3:1)

But if we hope for what we do not yet have, we wait for it patiently.

(Romans 8:25)

Add Any Other Bible Verse that the Lord has Impressed upon your Heart

Part Five
Kindness is Love in Motion

Kindness: A Moment to Reflect

Kindness is where love is expressed. Before words are spoken, before actions are noticed, and even before it is returned, kindness is already at work; quietly softening the heart. As you've just read, a mother's kindness reflects something far deeper: the gentle nature of God Himself.

This kind of kindness is not only felt, it is chosen. It grows in the small moments, is revealed through every interaction, and deepens each time you allow God to lead your response. It shows up in the tone of your voice, the tenderness in your actions, and the grace you extend when it isn't easy. This is the evidence of His kindness flowing through you, shaping your heart and touching the lives of those around you.

Choose kindness intentionally every day this week—even when it's not easy. Kindness is not proven in convenient moments, but in the small, unseen ones. This week, let your kindness be intentional, not conditional.

Below are your challenges for this week. You have seven days to complete them in any order. Place a check when you have completed the following tasks:

☐ Give each of your children one day this week off from their chores. Take that responsibility on yourself as a way to show love and appreciation.

☐ Give your child(ren) extra hugs and/or kind words for the entire week. Let them know what they mean to you.

☐ Make it a point to show kindness to someone who is struggling or making mistakes. A smile and a kind gesture goes a long way.

Remember to be intentional and **Focus Daily**.

Day 1 – Speak Gently

Mindful words soothes temperaments.
Replace harshness with softness and care.

Day 2 – Think before Speaking

When irritation stirs emotions… pause.
Respond with kindness instead of impulse.

Day 3 – Serve with Genuine Intentions

Do something thoughtful for your child today.
Let kindness be your first response.

Day 4 – Show Care Through Actions

Offer a helping hand, a warm touch, or a thoughtful gesture.
Let your kindness be seen and felt.

Day 5 – Extend Grace Quickly

Release frustration and choose understanding.
Don't let small moments harden your heart.

Day 6 – See Through God's Eyes

Ask: "What might they need right now?"
Choose empathy over quick corrections.

Day 7 – Reflect + Reset

Look back over your week.
Where did kindness flow? Where was it challenged?

From the Book —
Reflection Questions

1. When was the last time someone's kindness changed the direction of your day? How might you offer that same gift to soomeone else this week?

____

____

____

____

2. Are there moments when kindness feels more like sacrifice than ease? What would it look like to see those meoments as opportunities for strength instead of strain?

____

____

____

____

3. How can you model kindness in your home when frustration or exhaustion tries to take over your words or actions?

____

____

____

4. Have you been kinder to others than to yourself lately? What would it look life to extend God's grace to your own heart today?

____

____

____

____

5. Where might God be inviting you to show kindness that heals in your family, friendships, or even toward someone difficult to love?

____

____

____

____

____

____

____

____

____

____

Heart Check

Now that you've taken a moment to reflect, allow yourself to go a little deeper.

Kindness is not only something we show—it reveals the true condition of our hearts in how we respond to others. In this space, be honest with yourself.

1. Where in your life has kindness come naturally lately? Where has it felt more difficult?

____

____

____

2. What situations tend to test your kindness the most?

____

____

____

3. Have there been moments where you responded harshly instead of with kindness?

____

____

____

4. Are there recurring triggers that make it harder for you to respond in kindness?

____

____

____

5. What thoughts or emotions might be affecting how you treat others?

____

____

____

6. Have you believed any lies that make it harder for you to show kindness (such as feeling unseen or unappreciated)?

____

____

____

7. What area of your heart do you need to surrender to God to grow in kindness?

____

____

____

8. Where do you need His help to show more kindness?

____

____

____

Life Application

Take what you've learned today and begin to live it out intentionally. Growth happens when truth is practiced daily.

1. Today I will...

____

____

____

2. One small way I can show this fruit...

____

____

____

3. Who needs this from me?

____

____

____

4. How can I grow in love with intention?

____

____

____

Fruitful Notes

Thoughts ♥ Ideas ♥ Doodles ♥ Wisdom

These are the truths rooted in this chapter. Return to them, speak them, and stand on them throughout your week.

Be kind and compassionate to one another, forgiving each other, just as in Christ God forgave you.
(Ephesians 4:32)

You brood of vipers, how can you who are evil say anything good? For the mouth speaks what the heart is full of.
(Matthew 12:34)

And over all these virtues put on love, which binds them all together in perfect unity.
(Colossians 3:14)

Therefore, as God's chosen people, holy and dearly loved, clothe yourselves with compassion, kindness, humility, gentleness, and patience.

(Colossians 3:12)

She speaks with wisdom, and faithful instruction is on her tongue.

(Proverbs 31:26)

Add Any Other Bible Verse that the Lord has Impressed upon your Heart

Part Six
GOODNESS is Doing What is Right When No One is Looking

Goodnes: A Moment to Reflect

Goodness is where character is revealed. Before it is recognized, before it is affirmed, and even before it is understood, goodness is already at work; quietly shaping the heart. As you've just read, a mother's goodness reflects something far deeper: the righteous nature of God Himself.

This kind of goodness is not only seen, it is chosen. It grows in integrity, is refined through every decision, and deepens each time you choose what is right, even when it is not easy. It shows up in the quiet choices; in your honesty when no one is watching, in your selflessness in everyday moments, and in your commitment to do what honors God above all else. It is present in both the seen and unseen acts of faithfulness.

Choose goodness intentionally every day this week—even when it's not easy. Goodness is not proven in visible moments, but in the quiet choices no one else sees. This week, let your goodness be intentional, not conditional.

Below are your challenges for this week. You have seven days to complete them in any order. Place a check when you have completed the following tasks:

☐ Take one day out of this week to volunteer somewhere or help someone who simply is in need. Take your kids with you to share in the experience.

☐ Do something generous for someone else without taking credit for it.

☐ Take the time to forgive someone who has wronged you or offended you. And/or help someone else to forgive. Let them know forgiveness is the right thing to do.

Remember to be intentional and **Focus Daily**.

Day 1 – Choose What Is Right

Do what is right, in every moment.
Let your actions reflect integrity.

Day 2 – Pause Before Reacting

When emotions rise… pause.
Choose a response that reflects goodness, not impulse.

Day 3 – Act with Integrity

Be honest in your words and actions.
Choose truth, even when it's uncomfortable.

Day 3 – Serve with a Sincere Heart

Do something meaningful for your family without recognition.
Let your goodness be genuine.

Day 5 – Extend Grace Quickly

Release frustration and respond with understanding.
Let goodness soften your reactions.

Day 6 – Lead with Compassion

Ask: "What is the right and loving way to respond?"
Choose care over criticism.

Day 7 – Reflect + Reset

Look back over your week.
Where did goodness show? Where did it need strengthening?

1. Where do you find it hardest to do good when you know no one is watching?

____

____

____

____

2. How can you demonstrate goodness to your children this week through action, not just words?

____

____

____

____

3. What does it mean to you that "goodness and mercy will follow you"?

____

____

____

____

4. Is there an area of your life where doing good feels unnoticed or unappreciated? How might you see it as worship to God instead of work?

____

____

____

____

____

5. Has goodness ever cost you something like comfort, approval, relationships, or convenience? How did God meet you in that place, or how can you trust Him to meet you now?

____

____

____

____

____

____

____

____

____

Heart Check

Now that you've taken a moment to reflect, allow yourself to go a little deeper.

Goodness is not only something we do—it reveals the true condition of our hearts in the choices we make, both seen and unseen. In this space, be honest with yourself.

1. Where in your life has goodness been evident lately? Where has it been more difficult to walk in it?

____

____

____

2. What situations tend to challenge your desire to do what is right?

____

____

____

3. Have there been moments where you chose convenience over doing what you knew was right?

____

____

____

4. Are there recurring patterns that make it harder for you to act with integrity or consistency?

____

____

____

5. What thoughts or motivations might be influencing your actions—are they rooted in truth or self-interest?

____

____

____

6. Have you believed any lies that make it harder to walk in goodness (such as feeling unnoticed, or unappreciated)?

____

____

____

7. What area of your heart do you need to surrender to God in order to grow in goodness?

____

____

____

8. Where do you need His help to choose what is right?

____

____

____

Life Application

Take what you've learned today and begin to live it out intentionally. Growth happens when truth is practiced daily.

1. Today I will...

____

____

____

2. One small way I can show this fruit...

____

____

____

3. Who needs this from me?

____

____

____

4. How can I grow in love with intention?

____

____

____

Thoughts ♥ Ideas ♥ Doodles ♥ Wisdom

These are the truths rooted in this chapter. Return to them, speak them, and stand on them throughout your week.

Do not be overcome by evil, but overcome evil with good.
(Romans 12:21)

Let us not become weary in doing good, for at the proper time we will reap a harvest if we do not give up.
(Galatians 6:9)

Surely your goodness and love will follow me all the days of my life, and I will dwell in the house of the Lord forever.
(Psalm 23:6)

He has shown you, O mortal, what is good.
And what does the Lord require of you?
To act justly and to love mercy and to walk humbly with your
God.

(Micah 6:8)

Add Any Other Bible Verse that the Lord has Impressed upon your Heart

Part Seven

FAITHFULNESS is Standing Firm When You Fell Faint

Faithfulness: A Moment to Reflect

Faithfulness is where trust is proven. Before results are seen, before promises are fulfilled, and even before the path is clear, faithfulness is already at work; quietly building the heart. As you've just read, a mother's faithfulness reflects something far deeper: the steadfast nature of God Himself.

This kind of faithfulness is not only professed, it is chosen. It grows in consistency and is strengthened through every season. It shows up in the daily rhythms; when you're tired, in perseverance when progress feels slow, and in the quiet obedience when no one else notices. It is present in both the ordinary and the challenging moments, sustaining your heart and guiding you through every step of motherhood.

Weekly Challenge *Faithfulness*

Choose faithfulness intentionally every day this week—even when it's not easy. Faithfulness is not proven in big moments, but in the consistency of showing up, again and again.

Below are your challenges for this week. You have seven days to complete them in any order. Place a check when you have completed the following tasks:

- [ ] Make it a point to follow through on what you say you will do this week. Let your "yes" mean yes and not later.

- [ ] Every task you do this week, do it with care and diligence, even those repetitive, boring tasks that are never-ending.

- [ ] Give your genuine time and attention to your child(ren). Actually listen to what they are saying. Don't brush them off or place a screen in front of their face. Make an effort to show them they are important too.

Remember to be intentional and **Focus Daily**.

Day 1 – Show Up Consistently

Be present in your responsibilities.
Even in small things, choose to show up.

Day 2 – Keep Your Word

Follow through on what you say.
Let your words be reliable and true.

Day 3 – Stay Committed in the Small Things

Do the everyday tasks with care.
Faithfulness grows in the unnoticed moments.

Day 4 – Follow Through with Intention

Finish what you start.
Let your actions reflect dedication.

Day 5 – Remain Steady in Your Responses

Choose consistency over mood.
Let your character remain firm in every situation.

Day 6 – Trust God in the Process

Even when progress feels slow, stay faithful.
Trust that God is working through your consistency.

Day 7 – Reflect + Reset

Look back over your week.
Where did faithfulness remain strong? Where was it tested?

1. In what ways is God calling you to stay faithful when you feel weary?

____

____

____

____

2. What promises are you still holding onto that requires trust in His timing?

____

____

____

____

3. How can you model faithfulness for your children in your words, actions, and commitments?

____

____

____

____

4. When have you seen God's faithfulness sustain you through a difficult season?

____

____

____

____

5. Is there an area of your life or motherhood where you've been trying to carry everything alone? What would it look like to entrust that place to God in faithfulness rather than in fear or frustration?

____

____

____

____

____

____

____

____

____

____

Heart Check

Now that you've taken a moment to reflect, allow yourself to go a little deeper.

Faithfulness is not only something we do—it reveals the true condition of our hearts in how consistently we show up, remain committed, and follow through.

1. Where in your life have you been consistent lately? Where has it been difficult to remain faithful?

____

____

____

2. What responsibilities or commitments feel hardest for you to follow through on?

____

____

____

3. Have there been moments where you gave up too quickly instead of remaining loyal or consistent?

____

____

____

4. Are there recurring patterns that make it difficult for you to stay committed or consistent?

____

____

____

5. What thoughts or emotions might be affecting your ability to remain faithful in what God has entrusted to you?

____

____

____

6. Have you believed any lies that make you feel discouraged, unmotivated, or tempted to quit?

____

____

____

7. What area(s) of your life do you need to surrender to God in order to grow in faithfulness?

____

____

____

8. Where do you need His help to remain committed?

____

____

____

Life Application

Take what you've learned today and begin to live it out intentionally. Growth happens when truth is practiced daily.

1. Today I will...

____

____

____

2. One small way I can show this fruit...

____

____

____

3. Who needs this from me?

____

____

____

4. How can I grow in love with intention?

____

____

____

Fruitfful
Notes
Thoughts ♥ Ideas ♥ Doodles ♥ Wisdom

These are the truths rooted in this chapter. Return to them, speak them, and stand on them throughout your week.

Trust in the Lord with all your heart and lean not on your own understanding; in all your ways submit to Him, and He will make your paths straight.

(Proverbs 3:5-6)

if we are faithless, he remains faithful, for he cannot disown himself.

(2 Timothy 2:13)

Whoever can be trusted with very little can also be trusted with much, and whoever is dishonest with very little will also be dishonest with much.

(Luke 16:10)

Be faithful, even to the point of death, and I will give you life as your victor's crown.
(Revelation 2:10)

Therefore, my dear brothers and sisters, stand firm. Let nothing move you. Always give yourselves fully to the work of the Lord, because you know that your labor in the Lord is not in vain.
(1 Corinthians 15:58)

Add Any Other Bible Verse that the Lord has Impressed upon your Heart

Part Eight
GENTLENESS is Strength Under Control

Gentleness: A Moment to Reflect

Gentleness is where strength is softened by love. Before it is noticed, before it is appreciated, and even before it is understood, gentleness is already at work; quietly fortifying the heart. As you've just read, a mother's gentleness reflects something far deeper: the tender nature of God Himself.

This kind of gentleness is not only felt, it is chosen. It grows in restraint and is refined through every interaction. It shows up in the way you speak, the patience in your touch, and the calm you carry into difficult moments. It is present in the softness that steadies your home and the grace that guides your actions.

Choose gentleness intentionally every day this week—even when it's not easy. Gentleness is not proven in easy moments, but in how you respond when emotions rise. This week, let your gentleness be intentional, not reactive.

Below are your challenges for this week. You have seven days to complete them in any order. Place a check when you have completed the following tasks:

☐ Make it a point to focus on how your words and actions affect others, especially your kids. Tones and facial gestures say more than you may believe.

☐ In a moment of tantrum or rebellion from your child, resist the urge to match their tone. Calmly choose your words. You have control over your own actions and your child can see your example.

☐ Be extra kind to yourself with your words and actions.

Remember to be intentional and **Focus Daily**.

Day 1 – Speak Softly
Choose your words with care.
Let your tone reflect calm and kindness.

Day 2 – Pause Before Reacting
When the unexpected occurs, step back and compose.
Respond with gentleness instead of intensity.

Day 3 – Lower Your Tone
Be mindful of how you speak.
Let your voice bring peace, not pressure.

Day 4 – Respond with Patience
Take your time in difficult moments.
Allow gentleness to guide your response.

Day 5 – Handle with Care
Be gentle in your actions and interactions.
Treat others with tenderness and respect.

Day 6 – Choose Calm Over Control
Release the need to force outcomes.
Let gentleness lead instead of striving.

Day 7 – Reflect + Reset
Look back over your week.
Where did gentleness flow? Where was it challenged?

From the Book — Reflection Questions

1. How can you speak with truth in love this week with grace, and gentleness?

____

____

____

____

2. What can gentleness toward yourself look like after a difficult day?

____

____

____

____

3. How might your home change if gentleness became your first response?

____

____

____

____

4. In what ways fo you see God's gentleness reflected in your own journey?

____

____

____

____

5. Is there a relationship, conversation, or situation in your life right now where God may be inviting you to respond with gentleness instead of reacting in frustration? How might surrendering that moment to Him change the outcome?

____

____

____

____

____

____

____

____

Heart Check

Now that you've taken a moment to reflect, allow yourself to go a little deeper.

Gentleness is not only something we show—it reveals the true condition of our hearts in how we respond, speak, and handle others with care.

1. Where in your life has gentleness come naturally lately? Where has it been more difficult to show?

____

____

____

2. What situations tend to trigger a stronger or harsher response in you?

____

____

____

3. Have there been moments where your tone or actions lacked gentleness?

____

____

____

4. Are there recurring patterns that make it harder for you to respond with gentleness?

____

____

____

5. What emotions tend to rise before you lose your gentleness (frustration, stress, impatience)?

____

____

____

6. Have you believed any lies that make you feel the need to control, react quickly, or respond harshly?

____

____

____

7. What area of your heart do you need to surrender to God in order to grow in gentleness?

____

____

____

8. Where do you need His help to respond with gentleness?

____

____

____

Life Application

Take what you've learned today and begin to live it out intentionally. Growth happens when truth is practiced daily.

1. Today I will...

____
____
____

2. One small way I can show this fruit...

____
____
____

3. Who needs this from me?

____
____
____

4. How can I grow in love with intention?

____
____
____

Fruitful Notes

Thoughts ♥ Ideas ♥ Doodles ♥ Wisdom

These are the truths rooted in this chapter. Return to them, speak them, and stand on them throughout your week.

Let your gentleness be evident to all. The Lord is near.
(Philippians 4:5)

Take my yoke upon you and learn from me, for I am gentle and humble in heart, and you will find rest for your souls.
(Matthew 11:29)

For our struggle is not against flesh and blood, but against the rulers, against the authorities, against the powers of this dark world and against the spiritual forces of evil in the heavenly realms.

(Ephesians 6:12)

100

A gentle answer turns away wrath, but a harsh word stirs up anger.

(Proverbs 15:1)

Therefore, as God's chosen people, holy and dearly loved, clothe yourselves with compassion, kindness, humility, gentleness and patience.

(Colossians 3:12)

Add Any Other Bible Verse that the Lord has Impressed upon your Heart

Part Nine
SELF-CONTROL is the Heart's Guardian

Self-Control: A Moment to Reflect

Self-control is where discipline is formed. Before it is visible, before it is recognized, and even before it feels natural, self-control is already at work; quietly disciplining the heart. As you've just read, a mother's self-control reflects something far deeper: the steadfast nature of God Himself.

This kind of self-control is not only practiced, it is chosen. It grows in restraint and is refined through every challenge. It shows up in the pause before reacting; in the choice to respond with wisdom instead of emotion, in the strength to hold your tongue, and in the ability to remain steady in moments of pressure, guiding your actions and strengthening your heart in every season of motherhood.

Choose self-control intentionally every day this week—even when it's not easy. Self-control is not proven when things are calm, but in the moments when emotions rise and impulses press in.

Below are your challenges for this week. You have seven days to complete them in any order. Place a check when you have completed the following tasks:

☐ Do not have your phone in hand or any other electronic device when speaking to others. Give them your complete attention. Personal connection is important.

☐ Read a Bible verse or chapter to your child(ren) everyday and discuss what it means.

☐ Learn a Bible verse or two with your child(ren) and reward yourselves to a treat at the end of the week.

Remember to be intentional and **Focus Daily**.

Day 1 – Pause Before Reacting

When emotions rise… pause.
Give yourself a moment before responding.

Day 2 – Guard Your Words

Think before you speak.
Let your words be intentional and controlled.

Day 3 – Manage Your Emotions

Acknowledge what you feel without letting it lead you.
Choose stability over reaction.

Day 4 – Choose Restraint

Hold back when you feel the urge to react impulsively.
Let wisdom guide your actions.

Day 5 – Respond with Intention

Be mindful in how you act and speak.
Choose thoughtful responses over quick reactions.

Day 6 – Stay Steady Under Pressure

When situations feel overwhelming, remain calm.
Let self-control anchor your response.

Day 7 – Reflect + Reset

Look back over your week.
Where did self-control remain strong? Where was it tested?

1. When was the last time youpaused before reacting and how did that change the outcome?

____

____

____

____

2. What moments most test your self-control, and how might you invite God into them before they happen?

____

____

____

____

3. How can you model restraint for your children in ways they can see and understand?

____

____

____

____

4. What emotion or habit might God be asking you to surrender so His peace can guard your heart more fully?

____

____

____

____

____

5. How can you celebrate progress, not perfection, in your journey toward Spirit-led self-control?

____

____

____

____

____

____

____

____

____

____

Heart Check

Now that you've taken a moment to reflect, allow yourself to go a little deeper.

Self-control is not only something we practice—it reveals the true condition of our hearts in how we respond, restrain, and choose our actions in moments of pressure.

1. Where in your life has self-control been strong lately? Where has it been more difficult to maintain?

____

____

____

2. What situations tend to challenge your self-control the most?

____

____

____

3. Have there been moments where you reacted impulsively instead of responding with intention?

____

____

____

4. Are there recurring triggers that make it harder for you to remain steady and controlled?

____

____

____

5. What emotions tend to rise before you lose self-control (frustration, stress, impatience)?

____

____

____

6. Have you believed any lies that make it harder for you to pause, think, or respond wisely?

____

____

____

7. What area of your life do you need to surrender to God in order to grow in self-control?

____

____

____

8. Where do you need His help to respond with self-control?

____

____

____

Life Application

Take what you've learned today and begin to live it out intentionally. Growth happens when truth is practiced daily.

1. Today I will...

____

____

____

2. One small way I can show this fruit...

____

____

____

3. Who needs this from me?

____

____

____

4. How can I grow in love with intention?

____

____

____

Fruitful Notes

Thoughts ♥ Ideas ♥ Doodles ♥ Wisdom

These are the truths rooted in this chapter. Return to them, speak them, and stand on them throughout your week.

Like a city whose walls are broken through is a person who lacks self-control.

(Proverbs 25:28)

I can do all this through him who gives me strength.
(Philippians 4:13)

Above all else, guard your heart, for everything you do flows from it.

(Proverbs 4:23)

This is to my Father's glory, that you bear much fruit, showing yourselves to be my disciples.
(John 15:8)

For the Spirit God gave us does not make us timid, but gives us power, love and self-discipline.

(2 Timothy 1:7)

For the grace of God has appeared that offers salvation to all people. It teaches us to say 'No' to ungodliness and worldly passions, and to live self-controlled, upright and godly lives in his present age,

(Titus 2:11-12)

Add Any Other Bible Verse that the Lord has Impressed upon your Heart

Part Ten
Bonus: When Fear & Faith Collide

When Fear & Faith Collide: A Moment to Reflect

Now that you've taken a moment to read, allow yourself to pause and sit honestly in this space. Faith and fear often meet in the most vulnerable places of our hearts; the places we don't always share out loud. There is no need to hide here; even in the tension, God is near, gently holding both your strength and your struggle.

Faith is not the absence of fear; it is the quiet decision to trust God in the presence of it. In this space, surrender becomes a soft release rather than a forced letting go, and the heart begins to rest again. Even without answers, faith can rise gently, anchored in the steady presence of a God who never leaves.

Weekly Challenge

When Faith & Fear Collide

Choose to believe God's Word every day this week—especially when it's not easy. If you allow Him, He will sustain you when you do not have the strength to continue onward. Trust in Him, even if the outcome is not what you desired.

Below are your challenges for this week. You have seven days to complete them in any order. Place a check when you have completed the following tasks:

☐ Memorize John 16:33 "In this world you will have trouble. But take heart! I have overcome the world" and Psalm 46:1 "God is our refuge and strength, an ever-present help in trouble." (If you know these, memorize two other verses that will build your faith in God.)

☐ Look up God's promises for you. Read them and meditate on them. Write them down in the Fruitful Notes section of this journal.

Remember to be intentional and **Focus Daily**.

Day 1 – Pause and Pray

When fear rises... pause.
Turn your first reaction into a prayer.

Day 2 – Guard Your Thoughts

Be mindful of what you allow your mind to dwell on.
Replace fearful thoughts with God's truth.

Day 3 – Surrender What You Can't Control

Release the need to have answers.
Trust God with what is beyond your understanding.

Day 4 – Choose Trust Over Fear

When doubt creeps in, choose to trust God anyway.
Let faith speak louder than fear.

Day 5 – Speak Faith

Be intentional with your words.
Declare truth instead of repeating fear.

Day 6 – Lean on God Under Pressure

When the weight feels heavy, don't carry it alone.
Let God be your strength in overwhelming moments.

Day 7 – Reflect + Reset

Where did you choose faith this week?
Where is God still inviting you to trust Him more?

From the Book — Reflection Questions

1. Where in your own story have fear and faith collided, and how did you sense God drawing near to you in that moment?

____

____

____

2. Which Fruit of the Spirit do you feel yourself reaching for most in this season, and which one do you sense God inviting you to grow in as you walk through your current valley?

____

____

____

3. What unanswered questions, "the whys," or silent aches are you carrying today, and what would it look like to place them in God's hands, even without understanding the outcome?

____

____

____

4. How has God shown His faithfulness to you in past moments of fear, loss, or uncertainty, and how might remembering those moments strengthen you right now?

____

____

____

____

5. When you imagine placing your child, your fears, your grief, or your unanswered questions into God's hands, what part of your heart resists and what part quietly believes? How might God be gently inviting you to trust Him there?

____

____

____

____

____

____

____

____

Heart Check

Now that you've taken a moment to reflect, allow yourself to go a little deeper.

This is a safe place between you and the Lord. Give yourself the chance to heal and let go. He will always be by your side in times of trouble.

1. If it applies, where in your life do you currently feel fear rising the strongest?

____

____

____

2. How do you typically respond when fear and uncertainty take hold—do you withdraw, control, overthink, or seek God?

____

____

____

3. Are there areas where fear has caused you to doubt God's goodness, presence, or plan?

____

____

____

4. What are you trying to hold onto or control that may be difficult to surrender to God?

____

____

____

5. Have you experienced moments in the past where God showed up for you in fear or uncertainty? What happened?

____

____

____

6. What truth from God's Word can you hold onto when fear begins to speak louder than faith?

____

____

____

7. What truth from God's Word can you hold onto when fear begins to speak louder than faith?

____

____

____

8. Where is God inviting you to trust Him more deeply today?

____

____

____

Life Application

Take what you've learned today and begin to live it out intentionally. Growth happens when truth is practiced daily.

1. Today I will...

____

____

____

2. One small way I can show this fruit...

____

____

____

3. Who needs this from me?

____

____

____

4. How can I grow in love with intention?

____

____

____

Fruitful Notes
Thoughts ♥ Ideas ♥ Doodles ♥ Wisdom

These are the truths rooted in this chapter. Return to them, speak them, and stand on them throughout your week.

The Lord is close to the brokenhearted and saves those who are crushed in spirit.

(Psalm 34:18)

So do not fear, for I am with you; do not be dismayed, for I am your God. I will strengthen you and help you; I will uphold you with my righteous right hand.

(Isaiah 41:10)

Praise be to the God and Father of our Lord Jesus Christ, the Father of compassion and the God of all comfort, who comforts us in all our troubles, so that we can comfort those in any trouble with the comfort we ourselves receive from God.

(2 Corinthians 1:3-4)

And we know that in all things God works for the good of those who love him, who have been called according to his purpose.
(Romans 8:28)

When I am afraid, I put my trust in you.
(Psalm 56:3)

Add Any Other Bible Verse that the Lord has Impressed upon your Heart

Part 11
A Final Reflection

As you come to the end of these pages, take a moment to pause. Look back with grace at your journey.

Notice the places where you've grown, the moments where God met you, and even the areas where you felt left behind.

Every word you've written, every pause you've taken, and every truth you've allowed into your heart has mattered.

The Fruits of the Spirit are not something you complete. They are something you continue to grow in everyday with effort.

True growth comes from understanding where you fall short. Continue your journey beyond these pages with the knowledge you have gained. This journal was only the beginning. The rest is up to you.

Heavenly Father,

Thank You for every moment spent in this journey. Thank You for the growth, the reflection, and the quiet work You have done within the heart of every woman who has walked through these pages.

Lord, continue what You have started. Strengthen her in the areas where she feels weak. Remind her of Your presence in both the ordinary and the overwhelming moments.

Let the Fruits of Your Spirit continue to grow within her, shaping her thoughts, her words, and her actions.

Draw her closer to You each day.

Let her walk in confidence, knowing she is led, supported, and deeply loved by You.

In Jesus' name,
Amen.

Closing Thought

Motherhood is a deeply personal journey of discovering who you are, not only as a mother, but as an individual and in your relationship with God. Along the way, life's demands, constant busyness, and unexpected challenges can easily pull you away from caring for yourself and your children both emotionally and spiritually.

But it is in the desire to grow; to seek better, to do better, that transformation begins. In that pursuit, you find the strength to overcome, the grace to realign, and the courage to continue forward with purpose.

May God fill your heart with His peace, strength, and presence in every season of motherhood.